Dust and Ashes

art for faith's sake series
series editors:

Clayton J. Schmit
J. Frederick Davison

This series of publications is designed to promote the creation of resources for the church at worship. It promotes the creation of two types of material, what we are calling primary and secondary liturgical art.

Like primary liturgical theology, classically understood as the actual prayer and practice of people at worship, primary liturgical art is that which is produced to give voice to God's people in public prayer or private devotion and art that is created as the expression of prayerful people. Secondary art, like secondary theology, is written reflection on material that is created for the sake of the prayer, praise, and meditation of God's people.

The series presents both worship art and theological and pedagogical reflection on the arts of worship. The series title, Art for Faith's Sake,* indicates that while some art may be created for its own sake, a higher purpose exists for arts that are created for use in prayer and praise.

OTHER VOLUMES IN THIS SERIES:

Dust and Prayers by Charles L. Bartow
Senses of the Soul by William A. Dyrness

* "Art for Faith's Sake" is a phrase coined by art collector and church musician Jerry Evenrud, to whom we are indebted.

Dust and Ashes
Poems

James L. Crenshaw
Edited by Katherine Lee

James L. Crenshaw (signature)

CASCADE *Books* •Eugene, Oregon

DUST AND ASHES
Poems

Art for Faith's Sake 3

Copyright © 2010 James L. Crenshaw. All rights reserved. Except for brief quotations in critical publications or reviews, no part of this book may be reproduced in any manner without prior written permission from the publisher. Write: Permissions, Wipf and Stock Publishers, 199 W. 8th Ave., Suite 3, Eugene, OR 97401.

Cascade Books
An imprint of Wipf and Stock Publishers
199 W. 8th Ave., Suite 3
Eugene, OR 97401

www.wipfandstock.com

ISBN 13: 978-1-60899-200-3

Cataloging-in-Publication data:

Crenshaw, James L.

    Dust and ashes: poems / James L. Crenshaw /; edited by Katherine Lee

    xiii + 58p. ; 23 cm.

    Art for Faith's Sake 3

    ISBN 13: 978-1-60899-200-3

    1. Poetry. 2. Christian Poetry. I. Lee, Katherine. II. Title. III. Series.

PS3602.A8427 D88 2010

Manufactured in the U.S.A.

To Nita, who is for me the closest rival to divine wisdom
(Sirach 14:20-27).

Contents

Preface·ix

I. Probings
A Scribe's Prayer ·14
Three Sacred Fonts ·15
A Fragile Presence ·16
Estrangement ·17
Beyond the Sun ·18
The Tear ·19
Pra[e]ying Mantis· 20
Cardinal ·21
Discernment ·22
The Fountain of Love ·23
A Conundrum ·24
Presence ·25
Spying ·26
Saving Face ·27
Two Repasts ·28
A Useless Gift ·29
Gideon's Legacy ·30
Job's Wife ·31
Jonah (Dove) ·32
What Job Might Have Asked God ·34
Not Yet ·35
Probings ·36
Defining "Fool" ·37
Music ·38
Anticipation ·39
Hope ·40
The Country Preacher ·41
Wisdom ·42
The Divine Gardener ·43
Coincidence ·44

Babel ·45
Forgiveness· 46
Childish Things ·47
Bamboo ·48
Mentors ·49
Methuselah, King of the Pond ·50
Kitty · 51
A Child's Game ·52

II. Sonnets
Imitation Pearls ·54
Falling Leaves ·55
Delayed Vindication ·56
The Recital ·57
The Touch ·58
An Obedient Mother ·59
Saying Too Much, Or Too Little ·60
Mental Reservation ·61
Compounding the Scandal of the Cross ·62
Nocturnal Revelation ·63
Burning Hearts ·64
A Divine Choice ·65
Sin's Spiral ·66
The Genetic Prize ·67
The Lure of the Familiar ·68
Passion and Compassion ·69
Hiding ·70

Preface

Dust and Ashes. I have chosen this expression for the title of a collection of poems because it accurately describes my situation as a mere mortal trying to believe what others apparently have no difficulty accepting: that the earth is governed by a benevolent creator. In this regard, at least, I stand beside Job, who complained that his friends have made him into a cliché, "*like* dust and ashes," because he dared question the dogma that the world was just (Job 30:19).

For some time I considered another title for the present volume, one that communicates the essence of a plea that best describes me: "Lord, I believe; help thou my unbelief," but I reasoned that my doubt needs no assistance. It's the belief that can use strengthening. So I chose "Dust and Ashes" because of the two places graced with its presence, Genesis 18:27, the story about Abraham's intercession for the doomed cities of Sodom and Gomorrah, and Job 42:6, Job's final response to the Lord who had, in the words of the narrator, appeared in a storm wind despite the irony of communicating from a destructive force responsible for the death of his ten children.

For Abraham, dust and ashes constituted his sole bargaining chip with the Judge of all the earth who interrupted his journey long enough to inform Abraham of his intention to annihilate whole cities because of the clamor that had reached heaven. The idea that God would bring suffering and death on innocent people horrified Abraham just as it did another loyal servant, Fyodor Dostoevsky, who has Ivan in *The Brothers Karamazov* state that he returns his ticket, preferring non-existence to such a world. That was not Abraham's way. He chose to challenge the Judge to abide by a higher ethic than the one leading to the decision to destroy whole populations.

Even mortals who are responsible for administering justice try to separate the innocent from the guilty, punishing only the latter. Surely, Abraham surmised, the divine assayer of hearts should measure up to standards to which human beings subject themselves. By merely articulating this bold thought, Abraham takes his life in his hands. Hence his subject posture when questioning the Lord: "Look, please, I dare to speak a word to you, I who am dust and ashes."

For over forty-five years as a university professor—the last thirty-nine of them at the divinity schools of Vanderbilt and Duke—and as one who has had several years of active ministry in small churches, I have continued Abraham's struggle to understand God's character, in my case, as depicted in the Bible, for I am not privy to private revelation. That flawed literary construct, a harbinger of unbelief for some, has brought constant agony to me, as the books and articles flowing from my pen on the problem of evil and innocent suffering demonstrate. Several of the poems in this present volume reflect that turmoil within my soul.

The fact that I am finite, a condition captured by the words "dust and ashes," means, to state the obvious, that my knowledge is limited. That much is a given before I venture to question God for all the natural evil in the world: the earthquakes, tsunamis, tornados, cancer cells, droughts, plagues, and more. Still, I cannot reconcile my belief in divine goodness with rampant evil on every hand; and biblical responses to the problem of evil, which I have examined at considerable length in my book, *Defending God* (New York: Oxford University Press, 2005), do not alleviate my angst.

In my heart of hearts, I am moved by the thought that somehow God has taken suffering into the divine being, the passion narrative bearing witness to that daring concept, also proclaimed in Midrash Rabbah which has God rebuke a celestial choir intent on singing praises while watching Pharaoh's army at the mercy of troubled waters: "My creatures are dying, and you would sing my praises." Such thinking, however, requires a radical change in defining God.

Although the idea of wholesale destruction, even on sinners, does not accord with my concept of deity, I take some consolation from the response given Abraham, the Lord's acceptance of the principle that a few just people can atone for an entire population. Unfortunately, this principle does not really apply in life as we know it; otherwise Hiroshima, Dresden, Constantinople, the World Trade Center, and similar calamities imply a dearth of good people on earth.

Then does the other text where "dust and ashes" appears ease my troubled mind? Job's undeserved suffering, and the death of his children, provoked far more than a curse of his birthday. The complaints placed in his mouth by the brilliant poet describe the human condition just as eloquently as do the laments in the book of Psalms. True, a person undergoing relentless misery may be forgiven for using extreme language, but its pathos lingers nonetheless.

Pathos aside, I do not think it possible to understand exactly what the poet has Job say at the conclusion of the poetic dialogue. If we could clarify the sense of the two verbs preceding "dust and ashes," we might offer a plausible reading. As things stand, we can only say that Job rejects (what, he does not say) and is comforted (or repents) on (or concerning) his finitude. If seeing has complemented (or contradicted) hearing, that experience has not brought linguistic clarity. "C'est la vie" in the poet's eyes is no small matter.

To be sure, obscurity is inevitable when anyone tries to speak about transcendence and its effect on the intellect. In any event, the poems that follow are inspired by my sense of finitude and by the unknown authors of two compelling stories about men of flesh and blood, men who took life in hand, in Abraham's case to rescue the perishing, and in Job's to make sense of a calamity that banished him to an ash heap.

These poems are in a real sense one side of a lover's quarrel, not unlike that describing Jeremiah's struggle to make sense of a deteriorating relationship with his Lord, Job's acute sense of having lost God, the lament psalmists' anxiety over a seemingly indifferent deity, and the extreme feeling of abandonment expressed at the end of the book of Lamentations.

Thankfully, the picture of the flaws in nature and their replication in society represents only one panel in a diptych. The other panel is brighter by far, and I have tried to depict it too. If the poems in this panel are few, it is because words fail me when I try to express the depth of my gratitude for all who have brought unspeakable joy to my life. The unspecified "all" includes non-human creatures—birds, fish, plants, and so many more--and humans. Together, these human and non-human creatures have made my status as dust and ashes anything but unrelieved anguish.

Perhaps it is natural that I am increasingly drawn to the book of Ecclesiastes. In it, the unknown speaker who goes by the name Qoheleth pronounces everything under the sun "utter futility" and questions the profit of all human activity. That does not prevent him from acknowledging something that may be in tension with the general tenor of his teachings: "For God keeps me occupied with (or burdens me with) the joys of the mind" (Ecclesiastes 5:19b). The ambiguity of the Hebrew participle *ma'aneh* corresponds to the two panels in the diptych that unveil my deepest thoughts. I ask only that my readers remember my beggarly status of dust and ashes.

James L. Crenshaw
Nashville, Tennessee
October 2, 2009

I. Probings

A SCRIBE'S PRAYER

IF
I were the pen
In your hand
I would yield
To your touch
And pour myself out
That you might
Be manifest
To others.

IF
I were the ink
In your pen
I would take shape
On the page
As you breathe,
Dancing
Before your eyes
For eternity.

IF
I were a page
In your diary
I would drink
From your pen,
Absorb your thoughts,
And mirror
Your soul.

IF
I were the cover
Of your diary
I would shelter
Your passion
From prying eyes
And surround you
With tenderness.

THREE SACRED FONTS*

Sacred altar and holy table
Join the blessed font
In majestic invitational chant
To which comes our twelve year old,
White robed, innocent,
Object of loving parents' gaze,
Who press one another's hands
And glance on him and back again
Where four founts beclouded
Pour forth droplets unchecked.

By what miracle cleansed,
This impish son under water pure?
The power of years ago
That took another drop
Lovingly placed in mute lips
And from it shaped
This fruit of pleasure,
Gift of prayer,
Can spread a rainbow,
Halo-like over these three fonts,
Staying the cloudless rain
Until yet another day
When the miracle of the holiest font
Grants new life to him and an unknown her.

*For Tim.

A FRAGILE PRESENCE

Clinging beneath a purple celosia,
The winged beauty finds shelter
From the scorching sun,
Oblivious to admiring eyes.

What kind chance
Led this token of love's wonder
To my flowers, and
Who guards this white wonder,
Suspended among predators
Ready to devour a fragile presence?

If only my garden
Were your permanent abode,
Then I would not search in vain
For you another day.

Sleep, my vulnerable visitor
From heaven's door,
And these eyes will watch over you
Till your metamorphosis is complete.

Then when my spirit
Breaks free from its earthly wrap,
And wends its way to a distant garden,
Will the keeper of that refuge
On seeing a fragile presence
Clinging to a leaf on the tree of life
Be touched by its vulnerability
To unaccustomed radiance
And protect it from harm?

ESTRANGEMENT
(Genesis 22:1-19)

The familiar voice that bids me
Go to an unknown mountain
Pierces my heart but stays the knife
In a trembling hand.

The deed's undone,
Yet the unspeakable lingers
Between me and Sarah,
Isaac and his dad,
The three of us and that voice,
Suddenly alien.

BEYOND THE SUN

1. Under the sun,
   the tangled knots
   of human carnage
   expose envy, greed,
   and bloated ego,
   their frayed edges
   masking a pained journey
   from trust to abuse,
   promise to betrayal,
   passion to indifference.

2. Above the sun,
   a master weaver
   twists diverse threads
   in many directions
   to reveal a pattern
   of hope and pardon
   for abused and abuser.

3. Beneath the heavens,
   victims cry out
   for measured justice,
   an eye for an eye.
   "A moment's satisfaction
   for past wrongs,
   finally avenged."

4. Beyond the sun,
   no one assesses guilt,
   or even merit!
   Forgiveness reigns
   in a kingdom
   that knows no end.

THE TEAR*
(Genesis 1)

Had God known the course
Of those first words,
He would ne'er have spoken,
Ripping night from day,
Land from sea,
You from me.

Instead, God shattered eternity's silence,
Then cried, a tear falling
From divine eyes into mine,
Exploding in a shriek of eternity.

*For David.

PRA[E]YING MANTIS

You watch from your perch
As I trim a branch
On a cherry tree;
Spare your life
After you have feasted
During a passionate embrace;
And contemplate the irony
That a single change of vowel
In your name
Transforms a worshipper
Into a killer.

Were I able to read your mind,
Would I detect a reason
For moist eyes
Other than indigestion—
A hint of remorse
From a searing conscience?

Fear not, fickle lover;
No rebuke will arise
In this one whose everyday name
Sounds like a precious stone
But whose conflicted soul
And tear-stained eyes
Await the Reaper's sickle.

CARDINAL

You fly from the feeder
To your mate on my deck
And gently place a seed
In her beak.
I watch you repeat
This loving act
Again, again, and again,
Until, together, you fly away.

I think about your namesake
Who sits in a seat of power,
And if he feeds anyone,
It is a stranger
Who longs for another
While the holy father
Walks a lonely path
And wonders what it is like
To be the object
Of carnal gaze.

DISCERNMENT

"Champagne for all my real friends;
Real pain for all my sham friends."
Those who live by this adage
Dare not sit at the table
Of Him who embodied a different one:
Prayer for the one who would harm you,
Forgiveness for all your enemies.

THE FOUNTAIN OF LOVE*

To the fountain of love
Now we bring all the sins of the past
To toss them aside,
A garment unclean,
But the heavenly Dove will descend,
Ever holding us fast,
As waters engulf
To cleanse every stain.
O the angels give voice
And the heavens rejoice
To see all God's children newly born
In the ever-flowing fountain of love.

Lo the heavenly door will swing open
And angels will sing
To see children wade
Where sweet waters run.
Come and join in the chorus
And praise God, for death has no sting.
In God's only son, the vict'ry is won.

O the angels give voice
And the heavens rejoice
To see all God's children newly born
In the ever-flowing fountain of love.

*A baptismal hymn sung at Clare Crenshaw's baptism, Vine Street Christian Church, Nashville, Tennessee. Set to music by Clayton J. Schmit.

A CONUNDRUM

If thought is mother
Of identical twins,
Word and deed,
Where did thought
Originate?

In human minds?
Then who conceived
Mind and heart,
Cognition and feeling?
If the answer is God,
Does the question
Go on ad infinitum,
Like the answer?

PRESENCE

I rise from lying in your arms
Throughout the night
And slip into my study
To begin a new day.

You follow me unseen,
Infusing every object
With inescapable presence,
Invisible and real.

My **Oxford English Dictionary**,
Defining my essence;
My Roget's **Thesaurus**,
Expanding my horizon—You.

My **Chicago Manual of Style**
Taming my wildness;
My Strunk & White's **Elements of Style**
Giving clarity and elegance—You.

My **Biblia Hebraica Stuttgartensia**,
Linking me to the past
And posing the question
Of the future—You.

My pen, ink, and paper,
Conquering time and space,
Exposing an inner world
For others to explore—You.

My desk
Yielding life's necessities;
My chair,
Comforting and uplifting—You.
My lamp,
Chasing darkness away
With the glow of colliding novelty;
My book ends,
Proclaiming love's exclusivity
And enclosing friends
In your embrace.

SPYING
(Genesis 18)

Banished to her tent
Away from "men's" conversation,
Sarah listened and laughed
Like a playful child,
Then, her spying exposed,
She lied, turning advantage
From pilfered information
Into rebuke from one
With X-ray vision.

Spared any need to spy,
Abraham listened while the visitor
Freely disclosed a plan to destroy
Sodom and Gomorrah without sparing
Innocents. Abraham's status of
Dust and ashes didn't stop him
From objecting in the name of justice.

Cradling a child of laughter,
The one whose dry ovaries
Produced the son of promise
Believed anything was possible.

SAVING FACE
(Genesis 38)

"Where is the village 'holy woman'?"
Judah's friend inquired, hoping
To recover personal items
Left at harvest time
In exchange for sex.

This effort to save face
By turning a transaction
With a woman believed
To be a common whore
Into religious devotion
Is trifling when compared to
That required of her.

Pregnant, sentenced
To die by stoning,
Tamar had to save
More than face.

Convicted by his own staff
In her innocent hands,
Judah tried to save face
By exalting Tamar
But indicted himself
At the village court.

TWO REPASTS
(Job 17:14)

A mother holds her newborn
Close to her waiting breast,
Modestly draping a cloth
Over an exposed nipple.
Drawing her baby near,
She feels the initial tug
Followed by rhythmic sucking,
Her milk flowing freely
Into the infant's eager mouth
Until, content, it falls asleep.

Except in primal memory,
No adult ever finds succor
Like that first repast
While cradled in a mother's arm.
In the end, memory itself fails,
And death makes mothers of all,
Ushering in an endless rest
Undisturbed by worms
That, oblivious to modesty,
Feed on cold nipples.

A USELESS GIFT
(Ecclesiastes 3:11)

If God placed *h'lm*
in the human mind
but denied entry to it,
what purpose that gift
except to tease
with endless quests
leading nowhere?

If mortals can't find it
from first to last,
in the interim
how should they busy themselves?
Trying to break the divine seal?
Gazing at beauty and order?
Hating life? Enjoying life?

At rainbow's end,
no pot of gold,
just utter futility
sans profit.
So says Qoheleth,
a wise teacher
under the sun.

GIDEON'S LEGACY
(Judges 6:13)

"Where are the mighty works of old?"
The words rolled off Gideon's tongue
When responding to an angel's bold
Assertion that he had long
Been the apple of God's eye,
Which he took to be a lie
Because hordes from the land of Midian
Had harvested Israel's fields of grain.

If Gideon's children today, overcome by doubt,
Had clearer vision, here's what they'd shout,
"God's wonders fill earth and sky:
Joy at the sound of a newborn's cry,
A wrinkled visage and silver hair,
A ruby throated hummingbird in midair,
Falling snow, a rainbow, a sunset,
Forgiveness's erasure of regret,
Miracles all."

JOB'S WIFE

In mythic Eden
a gentle breath livens
images of their maker,
an evening breeze
leaving behind
a divine rebuke
of sexually awakened
man and wife.

Outside the garden
the *rûach* as spirit
empowers prophets and warriors
but spreads havoc
among the innocent
as restless wind.

In Job's land of Uz
a senseless wager
unleashes a storm,
brings down a house
on seven sons
and three daughters
for nothing.

Beside the ash heap
her words are plain:
"Curse God and die,"
though she is deemed
fool and devil's advocate.

Shamed for loving too much,
unwilling to bless a murderer,
Job's wife takes no solace
from the double meanings
of *rûach* and *bārak*
(spirit/wind; bless/curse).

JONAH (DOVE)

1.   Preach in Nineveh?
    You're joking, right?
    Risk my neck
    For womb-splitters,
    Offer pardon from an avenger?
    "In forty days
    Nineveh will be overturned."
    Why wait? Guilt's certain.
    Bring it now.
    Then I'll praise you,
    Laud your fairness.
    I'll not assist you
    In miscarrying justice.
    Better to flee
    Beyond your reach
    Than serve an unjust master.

2.   Preach in Nineveh?
    Better than raging sea
    Or the belly of a fish,
    Sickened by an uninvited guest.
    I'll proclaim your word,
    Watch forty days,
    Hope for the worst,
    Pray no one listens
    To a reluctant prophet.

3.   My prayer's unanswered;
    You heard theirs,
    Then sheathed your sword.
    Better to die
    Than be seen
    A false prophet,
    Or lose faith
    In your fairness.
    God, the sun's hot,
    Like my thoughts.
    What I'd give for shade
    As I breathe my last.

Well, you care after all.
Thanks for the bush.

4. What do I get
For persuasive preaching?
An overturned bush
And stifling heat.
You bet I should fume;
You've violated a principle
At the center of the universe.
"On the hawk
Let punishment fall,
Not on the dove."

WHAT JOB MIGHT HAVE ASKED GOD

Have you
    seen a child's mangled body,
    crushed like an ant
    under a workman's boot?

Have you
    Felt the ache of a mother's womb,
    Emptied for naught?

Have you
    surveyed tangled ruins
    scattered by twisters
    while children slept,
    their last words
    hollow as a broken promise:
    "Now I lay me down to sleep;
    I pray thee, Lord, my soul to keep"?

Have you
    heard the screams
    of drowning victims
    when tidal waves rushed
    through dikes into streets
    once awash with life?

Have you
    traced the path of lightning bolt
    from golfer's head
    to smoking shoes?

Yet
    yours, the restless wind;
    yours, too, the raging waters
    and the thunder bolt.

NOT YET

"It is finished." This, or something similar,
The Teacher spoke through parched lips,
Nature bearing witness.
Who am I to question either, or both?

Yet my eyes still observe
The sting in death's tail
And tears of children
Mingling with those of the aged.

If salvation has dawned,
Why the persistent "Not yet?"
Mary's question
"How can this be?"
Has become mine.
Should I not demand
That creeds be truthful?

Anticipation of future union
Fuels ardor in lovers,
But can unyielding Mystery
Kindle a lifeless spirit?

In the uncertain zone
Between "Not yet" and "Now,"
I am like a young lover
Harboring dis-ease and hope.

PROBINGS

Prayer: the soul's searchlight
Religion: looking for a worthy recipient of gratitude
Truth: what divides and unites
Beauty: a reflection of inner being
Art: kaleidoscopic excerpts
Music: echoes of the heart's rhythm
Wisdom: questioning your own conclusions
Politics: open competition between public service and self-aggrandizement
Virtue: an intangible to which we cling reluctantly
Friend: one who does you no harm
Heaven: the potential of the present
Hell: regret for things done and things not done
Sex: a path leading either to the sublime or to a morass

DEFINING "FOOL"
(Psalms 10:4; 14:1; 53:2)

A biblical definition:
A fool says in his heart,
"There is no God."

A secularist definition:
A fool believes intelligent design
Initiated the Big Bang.

Another possibility:
A fool thinks he knows
Which of the two is right.

MUSIC

A hidden Treasure lacked
Only one thing: admiration.
So God created a world
Reflecting his glory
And gave a voice
To his likeness below
So they and a celestial choir
Could sing his praise.

ANTICIPATION

For every tick, there's a tock,
Every beginning, an ending.
If time stops on a tick,
Does all hope disappear?
If time's on a straight line,
Is there a mid point,
An intersection of a cross?

HOPE

A seed sprouting,
a blue pregnancy test,
increased bone density,
children laughing,
contact from an old friend,
the aroma of freshly baked bread,
a yank on a fisherman's line,
the rising sun,
birds at mating time,
a heart in rhythm,
undisturbed sleep,
freedom from want,
a beloved's smile,
an agile mind,
a reliable memory,
purpose,
Being.

THE COUNTRY PREACHER*

An ordinary man
trying to do what was right
and cause no harm,
he couldn't defend his call,
the inner resolve to bring hope
to the needy: nourishment, clothing, shelter.

He didn't know much about theology,
not even that Hebrew script
ran from right to left,
or that Jesus may have spoken
both Greek and Aramaic.

He possessed no silver tongue,
spoke plain words for simple people,
talking with them and their Maker
as friend to friend.

He shared the joys and grief
of those he baptized, married, buried,
friends who knew him simply as
"Brother."

*In memory of my father's dream.

WISDOM

First in time, pre-eminent in rank,
Wisdom watched while the Creator lit
The night sky with celestial fireworks,
By their light laying foundations
Deep in turbulent waters beneath the
Earth with its teeming creatures subject
To likenesses of the master craftsman,
Then lifted her voice in joyous praise
Of the maker of heaven and earth.

Among the newly created she chose to dwell,
Mediating knowledge of the Infinite
To humble God-fearers with open minds,
In time becoming a written word,
A sacred text, where everyone who
Understands the mystery of letters
Can read divine instruction
Alongside the Book of Nature
Written by the finger of God.

THE DIVINE GARDENER

From gardens come our basic needs:
For the table, vegetables, fruit, nuts, herbs;
For pleasure, perfumes; roots for healing.
So God placed the first couple in Eden
Instead of on a scenic mountain peak
Or beside the rolling sea, but
With people things seldom go as planned.

A serpent's agile mind and clever speech
Sowed suspicion and brought a curse
That robbed paradise of the present tense.

Now God patiently works the fields
With the offspring of rebels as seeds,
Scattering them according to their nature.
The weak, needing help, fall on fertile soil;
The strong, thinking themselves self-sufficient,
Land among stones and learn humility.

COINCIDENCE
(Ruth 2:3)

Scripture's "Chance" brought Ruth
At long last to Boaz's grain field
And more. That "and more"
Leaves the question unanswered:
"Does a hidden hand ever
Change happenstance to providence?"

The unknown author of Ecclesiastes
Believed that a single chance
Befell one and all, human and beast.
If he can be trusted, the
Answer is an emphatic "No."

What, then, should we call a
Moment when both time and place
Meet precisely, a hero rising
To rescue someone in peril?
Coincidence? Serendipity?
PROVIDENCE.

BABEL
(Genesis 11:1-9)

One language and a single goal
Might have led to heaven's door
Except for a restless soul
Inflated, needing more—
Equality with the One
Without any equal
Above or under the sun—
Who reduced speech to babble.

At Pentecost, Christians, united,
Understood a new grammar;
As one body they fed
On manna from afar.

How did we get from there
To casting dogmatic bricks
At brother and sister who share
A common heritage, a mix
Of good and bad? Have we
Rebuilt the tower of Babel
Thinking ideas hardly
Different from ours evil?

What if God's true desire
Is not about doctrine
But that we aspire
To live in harmony again?

FORGIVENESS

"I forgive you." Simple words that
Transform both wronged and offender,
Though hard to speak, are sweet
As honey to one who rues misdeeds.

A pampered, deeply hurt, Joseph,
Driven far from kith and kin
By jealous, treacherous siblings
Emerged from prison to occupy
A seat of high authority
But chose reconciliation
Over harsh revenge.

In still another time and place
A father ran to greet a wayward son
With open arms and threw a party
That riled an older son
Who valued a principle of merit
Above a healed family.

CHILDISH THINGS*
(I Corinthians 13:11)

"Once you are an adult,
Throw off childish things,"
The Apostle urged those
Who preferred infant's food
To adult fare.

Things cast aside
Return when provoked
By scent, word, and image.

A boy and his brother
Scoop clay from a stream bed,
Mold it into desired shapes—
An automobile, an airplane--, and
Let them harden in the sun
Into toys in which
They and their sisters
Travel to places unknown
In locomotion of their own devising.

Sooner forget my name
Than these memories
Of childhood imagination.

*For Martha and Nancy.

BAMBOO

Giant bamboo near a garden
Offers protection for song birds,
Privacy for humans, while
Unseen roots rush,
Like subway trains, their
Shoots reaching for sunlight,
Invading delicate flowers
And defeating all attempts
To contain the interloper.

Tiny transgressions take root
Within those bearing the divine image
And, between dawn and dusk,
Form permanent paths
Hidden from sight.
From these, shoots rise,
Best nipped early
Lest they become
Resistant to pruning.

MENTORS

Masters of trades
bring dormant eras to life,
conversing with ancients
and living among them
as sojourners from another time.

Apprentices of creative imagination
sit in awe
at the recovery of voices
from unearthed texts
in a language
silenced by time,
and dream of a day
when they can achieve
what seems impossible.

Mentors recognize
that they may be talking to themselves
rather than spanning the chasm
separating now and then,
but this awareness
does not keep them
from basking in admiration,
their reward from a society that values
purveyors of banal entertainment.

METHUSELAH, KING OF THE POND

By advantage of age and size,
You ruled the creatures in my pond,
Eating the slow, threatening others,
Until I arrived as a rival,
Forcing you to adopt
New strategies to survive.

For six seasons you eluded me,
Shaking free of the hooks
Or breaking my line.
Triumphant, you leapt out of the water
And laughed, or so I thought.

Then your luck changed,
Due to pride, carelessness, or fate.
The hooks held securely
While you pulled me about the pond,
Unable to surface and free yourself.

Lying in the bottom of my boat,
Subjected to tape measure and camera,
You seemed to plead with me
Not to hang you on a wall
As proof of my victory.

I lifted you gently,
Placed you in the water
Until you regained strength and
With a mighty surge, swam away.

This time I detected no laughter.
Just respect for a worthy foe
Now recognized as friend.

KITTY

She had no name because the one I chose,
Paw White, was nixed by wife and sons as in-
Appropriate for royalty. That's why
She came, or not, on hearing, "Here, Kitty."
When young, she loved to play with ball and twine,
At times to pounce atop my pet rabbit,
Who jumped ahead but not beyond her reach,
Then tired of teasing antics, bored, she soon
Began to look for food, a bed, a nap.
She birthed her young alone and cared for them
Until we found fine homes where they could thrive.
When old, she couldn't jump onto my chair;
Her eyes conveyed the pain arthritic joints
Brought on. I gently lifted her and placed
Her just below my lamp to ease her aches.
Too soon she breathed her last and saddened me.
'Twas then I knew I should have named her "JOY."

A CHILD'S GAME
(Exodus 3:14; Isaiah 45:15)

Hiding your identity in different names
That drop hints like players of charades
Where the group most adept at games
Puts the clues together and parades
Its intelligence, you invite us to decipher
The mystery of four consonants and a clause
Revealed to your servant Moses in answer
To his request. We play a guessing game, because
The Hebrew verb is sufficiently ambiguous
To indicate your abiding presence, continuous
Existence eons before any concept of time
And the cause of everything, the prime
Mover. None of these ideas is concrete
Enough for either children or adults to greet
With open arms. No wonder Isaiah said
You are one who hides. Should he
Have added that you are completely
Happy when adults, even reluctantly, are led
By the hand and introduced to a child's game?

II. Sonnets

IMITATION PEARLS

Visibly no larger than a single pearl
On a string adorning a woman's neck
While drawing admirers' gaze away
From natural beauty, and looking much
Like the gem, the cancer spread silently to
Facial bone so that, on its removal, the
Surgeon's hands had to work magic. Angry
Over its missing sister, other cells lying in
Wait after finding a welcoming site
Attacked their host like fire ants
Devouring a grub, scarring both skin and
Psyche. These unstrung pearls, not
Mixed in sand and sea, worked unseen,
Leaving behind a marred visage.

FALLING LEAVES

In contemplation of standing naked before God,
The sugar maple casts off its clothing,
Bright red leaves falling alongside pale yellows,
Passing greens near the ground still clinging to
Branches like timid children clutching their
Security blankets. Preserving modesty, the sun averts its
Glance till the tree is clothed again.
Time, the alterer of everything finite,
Changes fallen leaves under the exposed
Skeleton into rich loam that will encourage
An awakened tree to reach for the sun, its
Branches sheltering birds, shading humans,
Who are destined to discard their earthly
Wrap, replenishing the soil below.

DELAYED VINDICATION

"From the eater came something to eat,
From the strong, something sweet."
Coded language that disclosed a clue
While concealing a trap, Samson's riddle
Proved beyond ruthless Timnite's ken
But opened like his bride's tear ducts
Releasing violence foreshadowed by his
Victorious encounter with a young lion,
Whose carcass yielded honey. What
Cost, playing with passion? Love's
Vulnerability exposed is every bit as
Destructive as Samson's slow descent
Into bondage, evoking a prayer for
Vindication. In due time, God sent John Milton.

THE RECITAL*

Sitting loosely on church pews,
Musical scores in moist hands,
Children not yet fifteen
Listen for their names
And hope to please nervous
Parents who wish for
Perfection, like the teacher.
Those attending the recital
Will long remember
Visual images after mistakes—
A faint blush, a shy glance,
A shrug of shoulders, a suppressed giggle,
A hasty exodus—transforming
The performance into celestial music.

*For my grandchildren: Elizabeth, Emily, Connor, Clare, and Carolyn.

THE TOUCH*

We walk on a greenway near our house
Hand in hand. "To keep from falling,"
We tell a young couple we meet,
Who hide their amusement on seeing
Seventy-five year olds defending a touch
On which they have relied for over five decades.
Keeping our hands apart, they realize,
Would be more difficult than recovering
Original colors from thoroughly mixed paint.
They walk at a faster pace than we,
Soon disappearing around a curve ahead,
But not before we observe the wife
Reach for her husband's waiting hand.
What, we wonder, will they tell onlookers?

*For Nita.

AN OBEDIENT MOTHER

"Mother's at the hospice—dying,"
My sister reported by phone one Christmas Eve.
The cold that blanketed me then and matched the
Ice covering the Interstate separating us
Did not thaw along with nature's fury
Until, standing over her frail frame,
I fed her spoonfuls of hot chicken soup
And heard her say she felt no pain.
As winter's blast has a way of coming back,
So her warm glow surrendered to the cold.
Kissing her, I whispered goodbye.
"Mother, you can go now. You will be
Better off in the arms of a loving Parent."
Reversing roles, the mother obeyed her son.

SAYING TOO MUCH, OR TOO LITTLE
(Daniel 3:25)

"Didn't we throw three men, bound, into the fire?"
Nebuchadnezzar asked his companions, adding
"I see four men in the furnace, free and unharmed,
One divine." Amazement, replacing rage,
Seeks confirmation of what seems beyond belief.
Faced with the implausible, we try to
Discover whether or not our vision is clear.
Thinking our intellect free of superstition,
We read such stories as symbolic truth.
If a megalomaniac saw too much, do we
See too little? Are divine beings accessible
To the naked eye, even against a sheet of fire?
How do we know anything? By report: "I've seen fire."
By vision: "I see fire." By touch: "I feel fire."

MENTAL RESERVATION

Religious finger crossing,
Spiritual mental reservation,
Lets one utter creeds
That, viewed literally,
Lack credibility.
The liturgy affirms
Unverifiable mysteries,
Irrational claims
About the sublime.
With muted voice,
Spiritual fingers crossed,
The timid join the bold,
Confessing faith-claims
For their symbolism alone.

COMPOUNDING THE SCANDAL OF THE CROSS

The desire to worship a supreme Being
Should not engender a sense of shame
Above and beyond the scandal of the cross,
But that is what I feel when the blood
Of the victims of religious fervor raises
Its voice to heaven and is drowned out
By the clamor of preachers' inflated egos,
Charlatans who bend Jesus' teachings
For personal gain and prey on the trust
Of good intentioned but simple people.
What convoluted reading of sacred texts
Transforms the demand to sell all and give
To the poor into a license for amassing a
Fortune by invoking a gospel of prosperity?

NOCTURNAL REVELATION

During the night, God spoke:
"Inform people the end is near,
Days never seen before,
Likenesses of Stalin and Hitler,
Armies always in readiness."
The evangelist reported this audition
As a daily occurrence, routinely met,
Then wondered why some believed him
Victim of self-deluded importance
That merges distinct realms and
Thinks one can see Infinity's
Plans for the future with clear vision.
Time makes liars of everyone whose
Certainty distances creatures from creator.

BURNING HEARTS

A shadow lengthens
On the hill called Calvary
And mourners head home
Unaware of a stranger
Whose loss God alone
Can comprehend.
The pall of crushed hope
Hovering over their talk
Lifts when the Teacher
Unlocks the secrets
Of prophetic witness
Before their weary eyes
And makes his identity
Known to burning hearts.

A DIVINE CHOICE

Goodness, power, and justice. If God lacks one,
Belief is bedeviled by the presence of evil,
Which in excess contradicts the first and
Corrupts the other two. When God first
Thought about creating a world, wise angels
Warned that justice and mercy cannot co-exist.
Favor justice, and his image-bearers
Face a bleak future below. Favor mercy, and
Strong elbows will spread misery abroad.
Faced with a dilemma, and unaware of
Sin's attraction to finite beings, the Creator
Believed he could balance the two qualities.
Time, non-existent in the heavenly realm,
Proved the angels correct.

SIN'S SPIRAL
(2 Samuel 12:15-23)

Children who've done no wrong
Suffer for sins their parents long
Regret. As King David learned, prayer
And humility won't save a single hair
Of an innocent. Unchecked lust rouses anger
Neither remorse nor payment in silver
Assuages. When parents lose sight
Of what decent people consider right,
Boys and girls lack a moral compass
To help them achieve a little success
At negotiating hazardous waters. They see
A pattern of waywardness, then hypocrisy
Hiding past offenses that, when aired,
Result in no family member being spared.

THE GENETIC PRIZE

The least-read section of local newspapers
Becomes the first page opened the nearer
We come to our eightieth Easter Sunday.
In obituaries we confront our own mortality
As friend after friend moves to the front of
The line and drops off, each one taking a
Piece of our heart. Perhaps that flaw
In Methuselah's longevity explains the
Shorter life-span of generations after the flood.
Loneliness, the result of many departures,
And wisdom, the gift of silver hair and
A wrinkled countenance, compelled him to
Ask that his Maker hang up the
Genetic prize for the good of humankind.

THE LURE OF THE FAMILIAR

The lure of the familiar conceals
Even more than it reveals.
Purists clinging to King James' Bible
As uniquely inspired have a viable
Criticism of modern versions' babble
That prevents memorizing entire
Verses that comfort and edify.
Nostalgia for the well-known
Leads some worshippers to decry
New hymnals, theologically smart,
As failing to touch the heart
And depriving communal singing
Of precious memories sown
Into the very fabric of being.

PASSION AND COMPASSION

The simple imperative,
"Be holy, as I am holy,"
Initiated a drama,
A sublime passion
Consisting of three acts:
A failed imitation of God,
A perceived moral gap,
And a divine substitute.
A cleansing fountain
And a sacred meal
Begins another drama
Of true repentance,
Blessed forgiveness,
And compassion.

HIDING
(Isaiah 65:1)

When the supreme act of self-disclosure
Introduces a name with multiple meanings
While emphasizing what is withheld
From a loyal servant, it's perfectly clear
That you are indeed one who hides,
Even though you express a desire to be found
And accuse your people of not searching.
If you really want to be known, show
Yourself and stop making the quest futile.
I've hunted you, like Job looking for
Hidden treasure and coming up empty.
If you'll drop a clue about your hiding place,
I'll search for you as long as I breathe,
Like a moth flying toward a flame.